The Perils of Geography

The Perils
of Geography

Helen Humphreys

Brick Books

CANADIAN CATALOGUING IN PUBLICATION DATA

Humphreys, Helen, 1961 –
   The perils of geography

Poems.
ISBN 0-919626-83-1

1. Title.

PS8565.U56P47 1995   C811'.54   C95-931960-3
PR9199.3.H85P47 1995

The support of the Canada Council and the Ontario Arts
Council is gratefully acknowledged. The support of the
Government of Ontario through the Ministry of Culture,
Tourism and Recreation is also gratefully acknowledged.

Cover is after a painting, *Spear* by Louise Andrew.

Typeset in Trump Mediaeval. Printed and bound by Coach
House Printing. The stock is acid-free Zephyr Antique laid.

Brick Books
431 Boler Road, Box 20081
London, Ontario
N6K 4G6 Canada

For Matthew, Kathy, and Mary Louise

1. Winter Aconite

Climbing

Up on the backs of hills, higher
than the geometry of birds. Distance
is a wrinkle in the smooth sky and the
sun behind the peaks leaves a residue of
red around the rim, like the glow
of a stove burner left on. Bluebells bruise
the slopes, grounded clouds of dusky
blush. The small, hidden lake,
scuffed grey, is an ear cupped
for the gossip of the screes.

Stop, and this becomes a view.
Take a picture. Look down.
Say, How beautiful. How high.
All a scenic lie. Up here it's
what surrounds not what's made still.
Not the postcard or the word.
It's the molten seam of sheep, draining
out of a ragged hole in the sky. It's
the time while you're walking
towards them, not thinking about
writing this down. The moving line.

Flick of a dog in the heather.

The Perils of Geography

Landscape calls landscape.
Each shiny surprise of roof
in valleys you don't expect
is the taste of rain when
you were young, mouth wide open
under galvanized skies.

The pulse of sunlight
sliding along train track,
shunting your heart into
sidings of loss, bumping
don't go don't go don't go
against the barricade.

Every misted hollow folds
words over on your tongue.
Like time travel gone wrong,
the perils of geography.
All that old cartography.
O, the New World.

Walking on Water

It's ten miles up the dry riverbed and
hey, where are you going? Legs gone crazy
with a memory of running that hasn't
stayed perfect enough to work again.
I'm flinging words at your back, hard ones,
at your too-big-borrowed-red-shirt back
and nothing's hitting, nothing's even close.
Don't think I'm coming after you (even
though I am coming after you). And hey,
I brought you out here to *walk* on water;
ten miles of dry riverbed that still
smells fishy when the first rains come.

Blurring

You are a teenager, up all night
with friends, drinking;
driving out too early in the morning
in search of breakfast. But
nothing's open and no one thought
of that and it's raining so you
drive up over the city to the *Lookout*,
only it's foggy and you can't see
anything so you don't get out of the car.

Sitting out back of your house
you're telling me this and I
have to go home but not yet.
We're talking moments of clarity
in the almost-darkness and your cat
is tied to the porch with string,
flops across the soft grass
like some strange furry fish.

Now I sit here, six days alone
in this cottage and raise binoculars
to track a flash of red between trees.
I see instead, across the lake,
a large man and woman on the shore.
Large woman points at something
in the dirt. Large man kicks it.

I'm spying on my neighbours and
remembering your story, thinking
that you never told me what it was
that became clear; or else I've forgotten.
All I know this moment is that
the magnified world is oddly disappointing
and the sun is going down here,
reeling distance in across the water
to break gold and sudden on
the shoal of shadow outside this window.

Ambush

We are driving slow roads
north of the city. Roads
that remember the weight
of this truck, the shift
of our bodies in the cab.

Low hum of engine
opens the throat
of a hot summer night.

Ten years of this and never
this. Sliding down a hard shell
hill and suddenly the road
on fire.

A gate of flailing orange
swung shut across the
grey and borrowed distance.

I think it's an ambush.
You a signal.
We both get out of the truck.

A bale of hay is burning
in the middle of the road.
Nervous flame fingers jerk
up under skirts of darkness.

Your face across the fire
is molten, smoke-sifted,
unfamiliar. The thing we
never say, the one that keeps
us talking, catches on these
snags of flame.

No one waits for me.
No one needs you to rescue them.

Around us darkness has stiffened
the trees into outlines, props
for a loose flap
of sheet metal sky.

For No Good Reason

You don't really like the beach.
Fish huts, blackened matchsticks
stubbed randomly in the sand.

All that hesitant water nudging
the hard-shouldered shore,
slipping back to safety.

You're with a friend you think you like.
Walking the tourist line from
car park to refreshment booth.

She bends to something you can't see
and somehow you're escaping.
Feet running a path of Away

across all this open Here,

across all This.

Sometimes what's unexpected in us
is what we want to expect. What
happens is ourselves, happening.

Winter Kite — Three Views

We run the snow of the frozen lake.
Our bodies sharp against all this horizontal;
boots threading through the rind of ice, sewing
a red flag of sky onto the hood of winter.

Your turn. My turn. Kite spool shuffled
from clumsy glove to clumsy glove,
the nylon square careening like a drunken bird
above our heads, reckless from too much string.

We bank against the careless white, looping
wide easy circles for the staid and single watcher above us,
red-faced with held breath, surprised
into believing we are here.

Ornamental Shrubbery

When the Italians still owned
the idea, mazes were knee-high
after-dinner decoration
for people with too much
tragic statuary and vague
yearnings for disorder.

Even Leonardo da Vinci
had one, wrote in his notebook,
"repair the labyrinth." Perhaps after
a guest, impatient with wine,
went butting through those
short-back-and-sides hedges,
trying to get out not in.

Leonardo
in the low Italian sun
of the next evening, walking
the dead-ends with string and clippers.

How does one keep anything
contained? What does the centre mean
if you can see it
from the verandah?

Being Shown the Garden

I'm just off the motorcycle, being
careful to follow you being careful
up the rows of sand and green.

These are the three kinds of beans.
These are the roses, scorched from no rain.
These are the beets the rabbit ate.

This is where the onions used to be.
(You blew them up trying to shoot
the rabbit). This is alyssum.

Clumsy from the highway I forget
to look down as well as ahead,
tread on something small by the tomatoes.

I'm still held on a sweep of grey
with clouds like torn paper
over the rise of Moonstone hill.

I'm still in the parking lot where
everyone stopped moving on asphalt
toward the thought of North

and leaned up against their cars
in bright, bright clothes; drinking
slow coffees, refolding maps.

You're pointing out the purple things
and I'm just stepping out
the truck stop door.

The parking lot is ablaze with
clusters of people.

Here are wheels of flowers encircled by sand.

Circumnavigation

The boat is sunk in
a concrete well, just
feet from the real sea.
Dull hull caught in a net
of rails. Masts, giant
pins to hold her here
and still.

Inside, white vinyl bunks
black with grime. Small
plants dried to algaed powder
in the sink. All the dishes
behind clear plastic shields.

It's history from my lifetime,
this boat and the man who
sailed her alone around the
world. I know the details.
That parched greenery what's
left of mustard sprouts. That
oven for baking bread.

The fancy plastic coloured plates
are my childhood ones. Those
books on the shelves stories
I grew up reading. That white vinyl
is the backseat of the blue Falcon.

Which is his voyage, which is mine?
What route around the world?
How not to confuse the comforts
of home with the perils of the sea?
The sudden displayed importance
of the plates, that flashlight,
those blankets.

Flood

In this high water, telephone poles cancel
their allegiance to trees and logs.

The thin crescent of road still visible
is a loose stroke of calligraphy.

Houses, inches from disaster. Corn sways
underwater. A cow is a decorative handle
for a shiny lid of mud.

There's no map of this. And no
talking on the bus. Black wire
hangs slack between everything.
What hasn't drowned will float away.
The river grown enormous, and gone.

Look. You can't even see the main channel.

Winter Aconite

There are words that sound
like the rain. How it
rattles an upstairs window
in a room where a TV
sizzles in the low light.

Late-night gardeners sway
in static, stand in mud.

    Gypsophilia   Sycamore

There are aerial shots of
a famous garden, and words
that don't sound the colour
they are when you
look them up later in books.

    Aubretia   Weigelia

The gardeners explain the dahlias.
Rain shifts loose petals
in the courtyard below.

    Lobelia   Catalpa   Ash

You thought it would help
to know the names of things.

Viburnum   *Asplenium*
Groundsel *Coryalis*
Amaryllis
Azureum
Spirea

Clematis

Rose

Landscape on a Birthday

All day the ground is
restless with mud, glitching up
into hunchback bubbles,
plotting the ruin of rocks.

Birds are sprinkled
against grey sky, specks
of black pepper flung
up to find the sun.

All day the wind is
a blunt hammer swinging
down the row of winter trees.

The lake from the window
a stiff blue arm.

11. Singing to the Bees

I.

Pigs can see the wind.

Down by the barn
the pigs are restless;
toss their heads,
behave like horses.
Skid through the mud and straw
on wild hooves,
snout-jousting.

At the fence,
nose pushed between
the wooden rails
is the sentinel pig,
the serious pig.
Waiting for the first twitch
of distant grass,
the long, slow tumble
of wind across the field.

And when it comes,
when that first cool slap
hits their skins
the whole pen
of grunting, sliding pigs
stills.

They stand aquiver on
stumpy legs, nostrils
wide, snuffle the new air.
As if the wind is a gift.
As if it is all
they've ever wanted.

2.

If an older sister is still single when a younger one marries, the
older girl should go dance in a hog trough on her sister's
wedding day to ensure she too will have a wedding someday.

She goes the back way.
Long dress skating the crest
of the high grass.
Navigating her best shoes
through a channel clear
of mud and shit.

She stops at the fence
before scraping over
the rough boards,
and for the first time
since leaving the house
looks up.

Birds, in the trees by the creek,
black tatters of cloth
pinned to the wind.
A slippery sky, clouds
skidding down its long curve
to collide with distant hills.

Then it's one leg up,
the fence trembling
with her weight. Over
into the yard
of the one farmer she knows
won't be home.

This time there's no saving her shoes.
The ground is pitched
with small tents of mud.
It bubbles around her feet,
sucks the hem of her dress,
tries to pull her down, down.

The trough is stuck with
bits of straw,
dried scabs of mud.
She stands inside it.
A coffin. A boat. She is looking
for land.

By the corner of the barn
the mass of pigs
twitch against the flies,
watch her carefully
out of tiny,
pink-rimmed eyes.

She remembers the words at breakfast.
What man would ...
The kitchen thick with the smell of bacon.
We can't afford ...
Her mother collapsed against the doorframe.
Almost thirty.

She takes off her shoes
and hurls them into the mud.
She moves her feet a little,
just a little. The bottom
of the trough is warm
with sun.

Pulling her dress over her knees
she dances the length
of the wooden box
and back again. Feels
strength in her legs.
The sun on her toes.

Knees high. Twirl. Bend. Then a
leap, over the side and she is careening across the mud, skirts
spinning wide arcs around her.

She is dancing for the sunshine.
For the pigs by the barn.
For the only name
she has ever whispered
into the dark's soft ear.
Her own.

A twirl, a bend, a leap;
both feet driving into the ooze.
And then. (No. No.)
A sound swung down on the wind.
(No. No.) Bells. From the church.
Thrashing the silence, stopping her
dead.

3.

If you hear your old shoes dancing in the closet at night you will
be drowned.

At first there are the ones you know.
The bedtime chant of dripping water,
bass complaint of fridge and furnace.
And then a noise that by its strangeness
anchors all that other sound,
pulls it up to silence.

From the closet, a knocking; no,
listen; it rises into rhythm,
a wood tattoo, a heel beating,
toe slap, creak of leather,
a tap, tap, tapping from behind
the louvered doors.

It's the old boots, the ones
with holes. The ones you liked
enough to keep, not enough
to fix. And listen, under that,
under that you can hear
a softer sound —
the tread of an animal,
bare feet on sand,
water on water.

The sneakers, all the pairs
of ripped rubber soles
dancing modest dancing
with the boots.

You are lying on your back,
arms stretched out, fingers
coiled around the edges of the bed.
Already you feel adrift from safety.
Already the darkness
is starting to swell.

4.

It is unlucky to be travelling on the same airplane as a nun.

On take-off everyone
goes rigid, a plane load
of stiff people
hurtling into the sky.
As if being locked upright
will help us if we crash.

We're afraid of crashing.

The nun has a window seat
but pulls the shade. She
orders fish for dinner,
doesn't touch the dessert.

We're afraid of the nun.

We watch her for a sign
of our impending death.
If there is such a thing
as god's will, she will
be the first to know.

Even though we don't
really believe in god we
are more inclined towards
god's will than engine failure.

We are stupid that way and know it.

The nun goes to the washroom
and we all panic a little
as she walks sedately down
between the seats, her habit
brushing our arms.
On the way back she
smells faintly of soap.

We're afraid of being afraid.

We're not bad people. We
have families who love us. We
have moments when we're kind.
We don't keep our bowling trophies
in the livingroom.

We are afraid that the nun
won't be afraid if we
lose our hold on the sky,
if we spiral down, dragging
a jagged seam of smoke
to the waiting ground.

We're afraid to die with
screams struggling out of our
throats, with the nun's
prayers in our ears.

5.

If you sing to your bees before they swarm, they will not go off
your premises.

What bribe enough?
Conjured from the darkness
of the stone house.
A bouquet of bright words
gripped in sweaty fists.
A limp flag to wave
at the rising hoard,
that box of whispers
in the bottom of the glade.

What bribe enough?
What curtain call?
When the seats are empty,
the aisles full.
When the pulse of night
is sticky with scent
and words, words, words
have lost their way.

What bribe enough?
What sound will pin
the wings? What song
will stop the song?

6.

At least one wish of the heart will be granted. The goddess of
mercy must not be prayed to but once in a lifetime by any
person, but that once she will hear and answer.

Ask for love.
Think of sex. Think
of summer, of heat;
of how the day breaks
into pieces, floats out into night,
leaving a clumsy raft of darkness
where lovers cling.
Think of love. Think of moments.

Ask for money.
Think of love. Think
of better clothes, of
talking, laughing, smiling
with possible lovers
in riverside cafes, in
ruined temples, in a
park in springtime.
Think of money. Think of beauty.

Ask for happiness.
Think of freedom. Think
of space and sky and movement.
Think of reaching into time,
moment by moment, drawing
it out, wrapping it
around you.
Think of happiness. Think of security.

Ask for love.

7.

Spectre ships can be seen before wrecks.

The early sea
still stuck with needles
of mist as he passes the headland.
Rocks claim the shape
of the coast, reach out in twisted lines
like arms trailing in the water.

He knows the old stories.
All the nights of lanterns
and waves, bloated bodies
on the sand. The kegs
of liquor shouldered up steep
cliffs, stashed in caves.

He's been in them, into
the mouths of rock, the
damp throats of hills
with their slimy air
and seaweed tongues
clustered black with flies.

Better, much better
to be sailing past the headland
in a boat heavy with nets
than to be standing in
those narrow-necked
old stories.

The boat was his grandfather's,
his father's, and now his.
Its paint is scabbing off
and he can see that
under the many layers
of the same colour red
it was once bright yellow.

Who would have painted it yellow?
He remembers those men, his
father, his grandfather as thin,
worn out, unhappy. He cannot
think of them as being young
like himself, as having
sailed in a bright yellow boat.

He looks at the peeling
deck varnish, the cracked spars,
the sheet of plastic nailed
over the broken cabin window.
He cannot imagine anything else.
Not a cradle of gleaming

yellow, rocking on the sea,
bilges wriggling with fish.
Not himself in twenty years,
thin and wrinkled, wheezing
on the climb from
beach to town.

It is early. The sun
pulls across the tops of waves.
He sets his nets.
This is the life
they said he would have.
This is the boat he was given.

8.

To eat white currants unexpectantly is a sign of happy tidings.

Just before darkness,
the orange light
shows a world still scorched
from the heat
of an August afternoon.

Five of us. Two
sets of brothers and sisters
clustered amongst shrubs
at the bottom of the garden,
waiting for something to do.

Before the dirt bomb
attack by the two
boys whose garden backs
onto this one, whose faces
we never see — just
fistfuls of earth,
dark stars exploding
the piece of sky above the hedge.

Before the water balloon fight,
where somehow my brother's
arm went through the screen
door and Werner
ran for his camera
to photograph the blood and
his father lost his temper deciding
who would pay for the glass
and no one went
for bandages and ointment.

Five of us jammed in
amongst the white currant bushes,
clawing for berries, getting scratched
on hands and arms, pushing
at each other; laughing;
as the night patches itself in
around us, black building on black.

Before we stopped
treating time this way,
as something to be snatched at,
defended, gorged. Something
to be waded through triumphant.

Before we started
waiting
for something to do.

9.

At a funeral people gash themselves until the grave is covered with blood. This is to strengthen their dead friend in his/her attempt to rise to another life.

We stamp this moment down,
this one that cried you silent,
lying stopped in ribs of earth
under the beat   beat   beating
of our feet.

We shake your name
at the sullen wind,
the six of us who loved you best,
the six of us
who knew you.

We pass it between us,
breathe it moist and cloudy,
roll it off soft lips,
rub it on warm skin,
hold it shining.

The knife we pass between us too.
Strike with one hand,
surrender the other,
slash the indifference
the keeps you closed

in the fist of earth
beneath the shadows
of the six of us who loved you best,
the six of us
who knew you.

We give you a fountain,
fierce with glory.
We give you back your name.
We give you the moment,
open,
generous as a kiss.

10.

The ones you go about with when young will be the ones you
will be travelling with when old.

At four in the morning
we would walk suburban lawns
to the donut shop
in pajamas and sneakers,
an astonished moon trailing behind us.

Before your mother
forbid you to see me. Just
before I never saw you again.

You would make amateur
bombs at night, explode
them in the empty schoolyard.
Once at two a.m. we rode
mopeds along the QEW from
Toronto to Niagara Falls.
You would make tiny parachutes,
attach them to chicken hearts,
film them landing in your kitchen.

Before I was thought too wild for you.

At four in the morning
the darkness is tagged with silver
sequins of mist.

Listen.
If you remember any of this
when we're old,
be there, in pajamas at the donut shop.
I'll buy.

III. Tosca's Lover

My Sister Runs

But I never see it.
No foot flap over black top.
No long stride out.
She stretches, before and after,
upstairs with the radio on;
fingers snagged around toes,
forehead bobbing above an ankle.

My sister sculpts
in the room that used
to be mine. Whenever
the door opens, it swings into
a hush of figures, sunlight
beached on the white table.

My sister draws her body.
Sitting with one leg propped
on a chair, trying to sketch
her toes. Standing between two mirrors
for that half-sunk phone cord spine.

One of the dancers on the wall
in the bathroom has her back.
A grey concrete foot rests
on a wooden plant stand under
a spill of green, her initials
scraped lightly into the heel.

Art and love are made
from movement. The way hands
are fluid, the body a shore.
The way something still
must be touched, because, it is
getting
away.

Kata

It's how you talk
to the big spaces
now. Your body
shaping an alphabet
of push and pull
in the stiff-grass
autumn field.
Spelling you out
to the sky, all
angles and confidence.
A semaphore of
certainty. This snap
and sweep of arms.
The way you
move. This
thing you do.

The Heart as Bird

You've got wings, sometimes you
think so. There's a loose furl
of cloud flapping in the wide sky
and you're up there, almost,
circling that empty field, sure
of the straight line getaway,
your faith in geometry.

You've got your eye on the horizon,
but you're really looking for
a place to land. The big bail
out. That drop overboard. This is
what wings are for. Swoop
and stall and snap them shut,
like the blades of rusty pocketknives.

Close them on the edge of winter
and come down to shipwrecked woods.
You've got wings. Walk out to the end
of the world. Stumble through the
white surf, down to where
the road curves

slow and away like a shore.

Motorcycle Lesson

Distance is narcotic, ride it to
the brink of stupor. Grit in your teeth,
cramp in your throttle hand. Pebble-shot
of bees and rough rasp wind. Take
the straight line through the corners.
Lie down on the tank going a hundred,
push of air against your body just like
skin. Sprung rhythm of the engine, a
metronome for your heart. Ride down
to the city limits, smell of farms
and scrape of wings across the flat
sky. Lean into that horizon like you
trust it, left hand cupped above the
cylinders. Rise of metal heat.

Transcendental Basement

Our house is sinking.
Our house a sudden wild space;
better than the swamp
across the road, with its squashy
mud grass, wet shoe smell.
Our house is sinking.

My brother and I stand
on the stairs, pajamas rolled
to the knees. Our parents
are trying to save things.
The puffy envelopes for the books
my father sells by mail. The
camping stove. A record case.

We'll wade down to the flood,
my brother and I; and I wish
we had an animal to ride
across, some mastadon or yak,
something big, furry
as a bathmat. But I don't
say this. And we don't move, not yet.

It's early summer in the middle
of the night. It's been raining
for a long time and this is where
the rain has gone, after it filled
the grass up, after it slipped
down my bedroom window.

My feet are cold, standing
on the third step. The water's
brown. Things bob near the surface,
bump against the staircase. My mother
is crying. My father is quiet.
Look, I want to tell them, *we
have a lot of stuff that floats.*
But I don't say this. And we
don't move, we don't move.
Not yet.

Elbows/Wrists

Our mothers arm-wrestle
at your kitchen table.
Arms rising like stems
from the brown formica
on a night so hot
the moon bubbles in the sky
and we run in and
out through the broken screen door.

Your dog is a psycho, wants
to kill us. Can only be stopped
by food and french translation.
We wave plastic wrappers, fling
bright orange cheese
down the hall, yell
Fromage. Fromage.
Tu chien diable.

Behind us the screen door
flaps on its hinges. Our mothers'
laughter is a bouquet
tossed through the kitchen window.
The dog barks from the locked bedroom.
You've got your arms up,
standing on the picnic bench,
you've got your arms straight up.

When You Weren't With Me

After you left I stood
holding the screen door open,
listening for your car
long after it was through
the farm and gone.

The last of the sun
flickered in the trees,
like candlelight, like
the wings of a slow bird.

Inside the cottage everything
was the same. Table
by the window. Through
the window the two chairs
side by side on the deck.

The faint shape of moon on the water.
First stars nailed fast to the sky.

When I rode out early
the next morning,
up the dirt track
and through the farm
there was no wind
to scuff the mist
from the fields. No
sound to open sound.

The world curled into
itself, like a dry leaf,
like a fist.

Five days later, coming
back, riding the motorcycle
past the farmhouse, down
towards the cottage, I had
four hours of highway
on my skin and only
your name in my head.

Five days and everything
had changed. Green wicks
of grass rose up
from the ruts in the track.
Trees had unfolded into flower.

I stood up on the pegs, leaning
forward. The lake flickered
through the trees
like a blue pulse,
the wings of a slow bird,

like the shape of your name on my tongue.

Here

The way the light
falls, what it touches.
Gardens on
the quiet streets,
when afternoon is soft
as breathing, slow
as slow as this.

Certainty of colour,
the sharp surprise of
blue under the beeches. The
open mouths of roses.
A small collapse
of the familiar, a shift
as soft as this.

The slow rise of love.
Memory of someone's face,
a sure and sudden gift.
On an afternoon as quiet,
as quiet as this, the
way the light falls,
what it touches.

The Wild Horse

It runs the narrow path above
a rough weave of sea — dodges
crisp-skinned tourists — white
mane threading the air.

Wild horse, you say, as we stop
and watch it plunge upwards
through the scrag. You won't believe me
when I point to the field of other
horses, the gap in the fence, tuft of
white fur hooked on the wire. Wild horse,

you say, and we stand there watching
the white horse stitch up the horizon,
joining the frayed edge of coastal park
to a shiny hem of sky.

No one rides or follows it. I'm
sure it has escaped; but I can also
imagine a time when wilderness
came without car parks and guidebooks,
when knots of wild horses untied
a line across the hills.

We stand on a rise by the cliffs,
people stopped all along the path
below. The white horse moving
fast away from us.

Wild or not it can still feel
what wild used to be. It can
still unravel. Not us, who shed instinct
for imagination, wearing the real inside
out. We turn our eyes from the
white crease in the sky, walk the path.

Halfway to the car you look back for
the far off pull of movement, until
it's almost gone. Wild horse, you
say. This must be where it lives.

Tosca's Lover

Someone calls for someone
from behind the warehouse.
Voice like a beacon.
That flash, flash
trying to warn you off the rocks
by showing them to you.
Safety or danger
but the same route home.

Someone calls for someone
and it's a long reach
lullaby, rocking me back
to a childhood cottage,
to a late night and
getting to stay up
to see Tosca's lover die
in black and white.

Stabbed fatally and still
singing half an hour later.
I couldn't outlast him,
went to bed listening
for his voice to go out
like a candle
from the other room.

Someone calls for someone.
That flash, flash
across the grey. An
open-mouthed moon. A
cut and paste sky.
Haphazard and certain,
like trying too hard.
The taste of your own
stillness, how it comes down
as something
in your mouth.

Love is only a willingness
for love. And a moon
that big is no one's.
Open your mouth as if
you can sing in black
and white. Open your mouth like
you're dying like
that.

Acknowledgements

Some of these poems have appeared previously in *The Malahat Review, The Fiddlehead, The New Quarterly,* and *Nimrod: International Journal of Poetry & Prose.*

The superstitions that title the poems in the second section of this book are taken from texts in the collection of the Royal Ontario Museum.

Thanks to the Ontario Arts Council Works-in-Progress and Writers' Reserve Programmes.

Thanks to Marnie Parsons, Kitty Lewis, Sue Schenk, Louise Andrew, Elise Levine, and Carol Malyon.

About the Author

Helen Humphreys is the author of the poetry books, *Gods and Other Mortals; Nuns Looking Anxious, Listening to Radios; The Perils of Geography* and *Anthem;* as well as the novels, *Leaving Earth; Afterimage; The Lost Garden* and *Wild Dogs.* She lives in Kingston, Ontario.

G. TAEUSCHEL